Original title:
Dreams in Bloom

Copyright © 2025 Swan Charm
All rights reserved.

Author: Olivia Oja
ISBN HARDBACK: 978-9908-1-4900-4
ISBN PAPERBACK: 978-9908-1-4901-1
ISBN EBOOK: 978-9908-1-4902-8

Serene Gardens of the Mind

In the stillness of the dawn,
Whispers of thoughts take flight.
Petals soft as morning dew,
Brighten shadows of the night.

Each bloom holds a secret song,
Sung by breezes sweet and light.
Colors dance in vivid hues,
Encircling visions pure and bright.

Time gently weaves its threads,
Through the tapestry of dreams.
In these gardens, peace is found,
Flowing like a tranquil stream.

Silent moments, deep and clear,
Open spaces, wide and free.
Nature speaks in gentle tones,
Inviting hearts to simply be.

Here the mind can take its rest,
And wander through the vibrant ways.
In serene gardens of the soul,
The spirit finds its golden rays.

The Burgeoning Paths of Illusion

Winding trails twist in a haze,
Where nothing's quite as it seems.
Shadows flicker, shapes distort,
Leading us through tangled dreams.

Every step hides a new face,
Laughter echoes down the lane.
Colors shift, ideas clash,
In this dance of joy and pain.

Mirrors ripple, thoughts collide,
Chasing shadows, lost in thought.
Boundless realms of vivid play,
In the battles we have fought.

Each path offers a new choice,
Cloaked in mysteries like night.
We stumble, rise, and wander on,
Seeking wisdom in the light.

Illusions fade as dawn arrives,
Truths emerge from whispers low.
Yet in this maze we learn and grow,
Holding on to what we know.

Revelations in Floral Dreams

In gardens rich with blooms and scents,
Whispers of secrets softly rise.
Petals open, hearts unfold,
Painting truths across the skies.

Veils of night drift gently back,
Revealing colors, wild and free.
Each flower tells a story sweet,
Of love and hope and destiny.

As dreams weave through fragrant air,
Butterflies dance, light and bold.
In every blossom lies a spark,
Of wonder waiting to be told.

Awake, the world transforms anew,
As dawn spills gold on every leaf.
In this magic, moments pause,
To breathe, to cherish, to believe.

Revelations bloom in silent hour,
Where beauty gives the heart a voice.
In dreams, we find a sacred power,
To blossom forth and make our choice.

Beyond the Horizon of Reality

Where skies meet the ocean's edge,
The stars whisper secrets untold.
Waves crash softly on the beach,
Unraveling stories of old.

Each sunset paints a tapestry,
Of colors that blend and sway.
Beyond the horizon, dreams await,
In twilight's warm, embracing play.

Clouds drift slowly, thoughts set free,
Imagination takes its flight.
Across this vast and timeless space,
We glimpse our hopes in the night.

Reality stretches thin and wide,
As we chase the shadows of dreams.
In every heartbeat, a promise blooms,
Beyond the stars, more than it seems.

And so we journey, hearts in hand,
With the universe as our guide.
In the depths of endless wonders,
We find the truths that lie inside.

Dance of the Silken Blooms

In gardens where the soft winds sway,
Petals flutter, night turns to day.
Colors mingle in a joyful chance,
Nature's sweet and gentle dance.

Beneath the moon's tender, silvery light,
Flowers twist and twirl so bright.
Each blossom sings with fervent glee,
A waltz of life, wild and free.

The fragrance drifts through the air,
Inviting all who might dare.
To join in this splendid display,
Where silken blooms merrily play.

When dawn breaks, a new page turns,
In the heart, the spirit yearns.
For the dance that nature brings,
A harmony of gentle things.

So linger in this vibrant space,
Let every heart find its place.
In the dance of blooms, let us trust,
For in beauty, there is robust.

Harvesting the Colors of Tomorrow

In fields where golden grains do sway,
We gather dreams at the end of day.
Each hue a promise, bright and bold,
Stories waiting there to be told.

With gentle hands, we comb the earth,
Finding joy, unearthing worth.
Crimson reds and deepened blues,
Paint our lives with vibrant views.

Tomorrow's seeds in the soil lie,
Underneath the vast, blue sky.
Anticipation fills the air,
With every grain, a hope laid bare.

The sun dips low, the shadows grow,
A whisper of change in the afterglow.
Harvesting colors, let them shine,
In every heart, let love align.

As twilight falls, we gather 'round,
In this feast, pure joy is found.
For in the dusk's soft embrace,
We weave dreams without a trace.

Whimsy in the Blooming Dusk

When daylight fades and shadows creep,
The blooms awake from their gentle sleep.
Soft whispers linger on the breeze,
As petals dance among the trees.

The dusk is painted with hues so bright,
A canvas glowing in the night.
Tiny creatures scurry and hum,
In this realm, where wonders come.

With every color, a tale is spun,
Of laughter shared and love begun.
Capturing moments in twilight's glow,
Where time dances slow, ever so.

The flowers nod with a knowing grace,
As the stars peek out to take their place.
In the whimsical embrace of the dark,
Light ignites, a vibrant spark.

So let us wander through this mirth,
In the blooming dusk, we find our worth.
A world alive with every sigh,
In twilight's beauty, we learn to fly.

The Floral Pathways to Distant Realms

A path of blossoms leads the way,
To realms where dreams and colors play.
With every step, a new delight,
In gardens that glimmer in the light.

Roses whisper secrets in the breeze,
While daisies dance among the trees.
Every petal tells a tale of old,
In hues of crimson, blue, and gold.

Through fragrant fields we wander deep,
Where memories linger and silence keeps.
Each flower a portal to embrace,
The mysteries of time and space.

As twilight beckons with softest sighs,
We find our paths where adventure lies.
The floral highways never cease,
In their magic, we find peace.

So take a step and follow the flow,
Into the realms where blossoms grow.
For in these paths, the heart can soar,
To distant lands, forevermore.

Fantasia of Flora

In gardens lush with hues so bright,
Where petals dance in soft moonlight.
A symphony of colors blend,
Each bloom, a story, each leaf, a friend.

Whispers of nature, secrets unfold,
In silent stories, their tales are told.
A gentle breeze in soft embrace,
Guides us through this magic place.

From violets shy to roses bold,
Each flower's essence is a world untold.
They sway and bow, in harmony,
A vivid dream of fantasy.

In fragrant fields our spirits play,
As morning dew greets the day.
A canvas painted with love and care,
In the heart of flora, we find our share.

Underneath the starlit skies,
The blossoms sleep, the world complies.
In this fantasia, hand in hand,
We wander through this vibrant land.

The Radiance of Tomorrow

With every dawn that breaks anew,
The sun unfurls its golden hue.
Hope awakens in the light,
A promise shining, bold and bright.

Dreams unfurl like sails in air,
Guided by each whispered prayer.
A future kissed by morning rays,
In its embrace, our spirits blaze.

Through shadows long and trials tough,
We find the strength when the going's rough.
With hearts ablaze, we forge ahead,
Into the dawn where shadows fled.

The tapestry of life we weave,
In colors rich, we dare believe.
Each thread a story, strong and pure,
In the radiance, we are sure.

Together hand in hand we stand,
United in our bright command.
With every breath, we take our flight,
Into the canvas of our light.

Secrets in the Scented Air

In gardens where the roses twine,
A fragrance whispers, soft, divine.
Each bloom unveils a mystery,
Secrets laced in perfumed history.

The jasmine sighs with evening's breath,
A gentle call from life to death.
In fragrant hints, the past appears,
Combing memories, washing fears.

With lilacs sweet and lilies pure,
The air hangs thick with love's allure.
Hidden tales in petals stay,
Softly beckoning, they lead the way.

When twilight paints the bowers deep,
The secrets of the night we keep.
In moonlit gardens, hearts laid bare,
We breathe the magic in the air.

From whispered dreams to twilight's kiss,
We find the joy in moments missed.
In every scent, a tale we share,
Unlocking wonders in the scented air.

Blossoms of Yesteryears and Tomorrows

In gardens wrapped in gentle fade,
The memories of seasons made.
Blossoms linger, soft and clear,
Each petal sings of yesteryear.

With tender hands, we pluck the past,
Creating futures, shadows cast.
In every bud, a promise waits,
Of dreams anew, of open gates.

The daisies nod, the poppies sway,
In harmony, they light the way.
With whispers from the fading light,
They guide us through the coming night.

A tapestry of love and loss,
In every bloom, we find our cross.
Yet in the soil, hope takes its root,
Sprouting life with each pursuit.

Here in the garden, time entwined,
In every blossom, we shall find.
A dance of yesterdays awaits,
As tomorrows open wide the gates.

Reflections of a Blooming Soul

In the garden where thoughts align,
Petals whisper secrets divine.
Colors dance in morning's light,
Awakening dreams, taking flight.

Winds carry stories, soft and clear,
Every breath draws wisdom near.
Roots embrace the earth's warm kiss,
In silence, we find our bliss.

Raindrops weave a gentle song,
Nurturing life, as we belong.
From shadows rise, the timid sprout,
Unfolding hope, casting doubt.

Sunset paints the sky with grace,
Guiding souls through time and space.
In stillness, the heart reflects,
A blooming soul, the path connects.

The Petal-scented Reveries

In twilight's warmth, dreams take wing,
Echoes of joy, the nightbirds sing.
Underneath the starry dome,
Petal kisses lead us home.

We navigate through fragrant air,
Each breath infused with tender care.
Memories flutter, sweet and light,
Guiding us through the velvet night.

Whispers of jasmine, tales unfold,
In dusky hues, our hearts behold.
Through fragrant paths, we wander free,
A dance of souls in harmony.

Candlelight flickers, shadows play,
Petal-scented dreams at bay.
In reverie, we find our place,
In the embrace of night's soft grace.

Secrets of Celestial Flora

Beneath the moon, the flowers sigh,
In secret gardens where dreams lie.
Petals hold the stories vast,
Whispers of the future and past.

Celestial blooms in twilight's glow,
Casting shadows, secrets flow.
Each blossom tells a tale untold,
Of love and loss, of hearts bold.

Starry nights weave this tapestry,
In fragrant hues, we see and be.
Gardens cradle the cosmic light,
In every petal, a spark ignites.

As dawn breaks, the wonders blend,
In every bud, a promise penned.
Secrets linger in each sigh,
Celestial flora, reaching high.

Traces of Color in the Night

In the quiet of night, colors fade,
Traces linger where dreams are laid.
Midnight hues in shadows cast,
Embers of daylight, fleeting past.

Each star is painted with a wish,
A palette woven, soft and brisk.
Moonbeams spill their silvery glow,
Illuminating paths we know.

Whispers carried on cool night air,
Colors merging everywhere.
In this canvas, shadows play,
Imaginary worlds on display.

The night wraps itself around our souls,
In vibrant dreams, we find our goals.
Awakening as dawn draws near,
Traces of color, crystal clear.

Blooms Beneath the Stars

In the quiet of the night,
Petals catch the silver light.
Whispers dance on gentle breeze,
Specters played among the trees.

Moonlight drapes a tender shroud,
Awakens dreams, both soft and loud.
Colors blossom, bright and rare,
Each a treasure, floating air.

Stars above like scattered seeds,
Nurtured hearts and blooming needs.
In the stillness, peace unfolds,
A tapestry of stories told.

Nature's laughter fills the skies,
In every flower, hope complies.
Though shadows stretch and darkness falls,
The garden breathes, and beauty calls.

So let us walk beneath the glow,
Where night reveals the paths we sow.
In blooms beneath the endless space,
We find our dreams, our sacred place.

Illusions in Floral Settings

Upon a bed of petals soft,
We find the magic, dreams aloft.
Colors swirl like whispered sighs,
Crafting tales beneath the skies.

Chasing shadows, lost in thought,
In hidden gardens, solace sought.
Fragrance lingers, sweet and low,
Painting whispers, letting go.

Each bloom a mirror, heart's delight,
Reflecting visions, pure and bright.
In every turn, a secret shared,
Life's illusions, carefully layered.

Dance with the wind, twirl with grace,
In floral symphonies, we trace.
The beauty lies in what we feel,
Illusions bloom, forever real.

Lost in colors, time stands still,
Nature's palette bends to will.
In floral settings, dreams ignite,
The heart's illusions spark the night.

Luminous Gardens of the Soul

In the heart of the twilight glow,
Luminous gardens quietly grow.
Each petal sparkles, whispers free,
Inviting souls to just be.

Colors merge, a radiant blend,
Every bloom, a faithful friend.
Nurtured dreams in fragrant air,
A sanctuary beyond compare.

Glimmers dance in soft embrace,
In every bud, a hidden grace.
Illumined paths where spirits roam,
In gardens bright, we find our home.

Here, joy sprouts with each new dawn,
As shadows fade and fears are gone.
In this haven, hearts renew,
Luminous gardens, pure and true.

With every step, the light expands,
Unfolding in our tired hands.
In lush repose, we find our goal,
In luminous gardens of the soul.

The Canvas of Night's Embrace

Stars paint whispers on black canvas,
A palette swirls in night's caress.
Each stroke a story, deep and wide,
In the silence where dreams abide.

Moonlight weaves through trees so tall,
Casting shadows, inviting all.
In colors deep, the night unfolds,
Secrets kept and tales retold.

A soft breeze brushes past our skin,
Inviting thoughts to dance within.
The world asleep, yet awake we stand,
Creativity flows like golden sand.

The stars are artists, bold and bright,
Creating visions in the night.
In every twinkle, stories flow,
On this canvas, dreams will grow.

With every heartbeat, we embrace,
The magic found in night's sweet grace.
In the quiet, souls take flight,
On the canvas of the heart's delight.

The Muse's Garden Awakens

In dawn's gentle embrace,
The petals quietly stir,
Whispers of colors bold,
Life's magic begins to purr.

Each leaf a story told,
In sunlight's tender glow,
Secrets dance on the breeze,
As inspiration flows.

The fragrance fills the air,
With dreams that softly rise,
Nature's art unveiled,
Underneath azure skies.

Gardens bloom with intent,
Awakening the heart,
Muses find their refuge,
In this vibrant part.

With every vibrant hue,
A spark ignites the mind,
The garden's breath ignites,
Creativity entwined.

Reflections in a Petal Pool

Beneath the willow's shade,
A pool reflects the sky,
Petals float like whispers,
Glimmering with a sigh.

Each droplet tells a tale,
Of moments softly creased,
Life's beauty mirrored clear,
In stillness, an inner feast.

Birdsong dances lightly,
Upon the water's face,
Ripples weave through memories,
In this sacred space.

Colors swirl like dreams,
In a tapestry of time,
Nature's verse captured,
In a tranquil rhyme.

As petals drift gently,
They kiss the surface bright,
In the garden's secret,
Reflections take their flight.

Twilight's Generous Blooms

As daylight bids farewell,
Stars begin to gleam,
Twilight wraps the garden,
In a gentle dream.

Shadows stretch and play,
Among the flowers' grace,
Each petal, a soft sigh,
In twilight's warm embrace.

The nightingale's sweet song,
Echoes through the trees,
While blossoms breathe in dusk,
Swaying with the breeze.

Colors deepen softly,
In lilac, gold, and blue,
A canvas painted bold,
With evening's tender hue.

In this moment, we find,
The beauty of the night,
Twilight's generous blooms,
A heart's pure delight.

The Blooming Canvas of the Soul

In the still of the heart,
Colors begin to sprout,
A canvas wide and bright,
Where dreams can dance about.

Brushstrokes of desire,
In shades of hope and peace,
Each bloom, a revelation,
In silence, find release.

Thoughts weave through the petals,
Crafting stories untold,
A symphony of spirit,
In colors rich and bold.

With every stroke that flows,
The soul learns to unfold,
Artistry ignites life,
A passion to behold.

In this blooming garden,
Each moment takes its toll,
Creating vivid memories,
On the canvas of the soul.

The Secret Language of Flowers

In gardens where whispers bloom,
Petals speak of love and doom.
Each hue a story, softly told,
In fragrant dreams, secrets unfold.

A rose for passion, bright and bold,
While lilies weave tales of the old.
Daisies dance in youthful grace,
In nature's heart, we find our place.

Violets sigh in shades of blue,
Telling wishes, pure and true.
Sunflowers turn to face the sun,
In their glow, our fears are done.

Orchids, rare in their delight,
Whisper elegance in the night.
Marigolds with golden glow,
Guide our paths where flowers grow.

So listen close to nature's song,
In every bloom, we all belong.
For in the garden's hush and sway,
The secret language finds its way.

Hues of Aspiration

A canvas bright with colors bold,
Dreams take flight in shades of gold.
Blues of hope stretch wide and far,
In every heart, a guiding star.

Greens of growth in vibrant cheer,
In every leaf, a story dear.
Yellows burst like laughter loud,
In joyful hues, we stand so proud.

Reds ignite the passion's fire,
Fueling souls with sweet desire.
Purples whisper of the night,
In every shade, our dreams take flight.

Soft pastels of dawn's embrace,
Paint the skies with gentle grace.
In every hue, a tale we weave,
With colors bright, we learn to believe.

So reach for colors, bold, and free,
In hues of aspiration, let it be.
For in this spectrum, bold and true,
Lives the spirit, strong and new.

Nightfall's Enchanted Petals

When twilight dances on the breeze,
Whispers float among the trees.
Petals close in gentle sighs,
As stars ignite the velvet skies.

Moonlit gardens start to glow,
Underneath the stars' soft show.
Night-blooming flowers open wide,
In their fragrance, dreams abide.

Soft shadows wrap the earth in peace,
As night's embrace brings sweet release.
The world transforms in silver light,
Petals shimmer, hearts take flight.

Crickets sing their lullabies,
As dreams awaken, softly rise.
In this hour of magic's grace,
Nature finds her secret place.

So wander gently in the night,
In enchanted blooms, find your light.
For in the dark, the petals gleam,
And guide us softly to our dream.

The Symphony of Blossoms

In gardens where the blossoms play,
Nature sings in bright array.
Each petal strums a sweet refrain,
In harmony, their souls remain.

The tulips sway in springtime's air,
With every note, they dance with care.
A lilac breeze hums soft and low,
In gentle rhythms, life will flow.

Cherry blossoms, fleeting grace,
Make every moment a tender embrace.
In every bud, a passion found,
In nature's symphony, we are bound.

Daffodils herald the day's start,
Each blossom plays a vital part.
Their colors burst, a grand display,
In vibrant chords, they lead the way.

So let the flowers sing their song,
In every petal, we belong.
Together in this grand design,
The symphony of life, divine.

Vibrant Hues of the Subconscious

In the realm where colors play,
Whispers of dreams gently sway.
Shades of madness, strokes of light,
Illuminate the silent night.

Blues of longing, reds of fire,
Echo the heart's deep desire.
Greens of envy, yellows of glee,
A canvas of what might be.

Beneath the surface, shadows creep,
Messages lost, secrets to keep.
Ever-changing, a flowing stream,
Dancing upon the edge of dream.

Each hue a thread, weaving fate,
In vibrant shades, we contemplate.
Artistry of the mind unfurled,
Painting the essence of our world.

In the depths where silence sings,
Unraveling what the heart brings.
A kaleidoscope of vivid sighs,
Where unseen beauty never dies.

A Serenade of Nested Blossoms

In the garden where petals lay,
Gentle whispers greet the day.
Each bloom a note, a sweet refrain,
A melody in sun and rain.

Layers of fragrance, soft and warm,
Entwined beneath a nurturing arm.
Roses blush, daisies hum,
In harmony, the blossoms come.

Violets peek through verdant green,
Notes of laughter, calm and serene.
Tulips sway in morning light,
Resonating with pure delight.

Wisteria drapes with grace untold,
Tales of summers long ago unfold.
Lavender fields, a soothing sigh,
Invite the dreaming passerby.

Crown each flower with love's embrace,
In the silence, find your place.
Within their hearts, every song,
Echoes where we all belong.

The Tapestry of Nature's Dreams

Upon the canvas of the earth,
Nature spins its yarn of birth.
Mountains rise like dreams in flight,
Kissed by golden morning light.

Oceans whisper ancient tales,
Dancing winds in silver sails.
Forests hum with secrets deep,
Where the watchful shadows creep.

Stars embroider the velvet night,
Guiding travelers with their light.
Clouds waltz softly in the sky,
Crafting dreams that drift and fly.

Rivers weave their stories bold,
In the tapestry of old.
Every flower, every stream,
Threads of hope within a dream.

Rustling leaves, a symphony,
Resonates in harmony.
Nature's voice, a gentle stream,
Intertwining every dream.

Softly Falling Petals of Hope

Like whispers on the breeze they fall,
Petals dance from trees so tall.
Each flutter holds a story true,
A promise wrapped in morning dew.

As they drift, they touch the ground,
Sprinkling joy all around.
Hope delivered on fragile wings,
A gentle touch that nature brings.

Colors blend in a soft embrace,
Reminders of love's warm grace.
With every petal, hearts align,
In silence, beauty intertwines.

Beneath the weight of dreams untold,
Softly unfolding, brave and bold.
A sign that life persistently flows,
In every heart, a garden grows.

So cherish the moments, let them sweep,
Through your soul so rich and deep.
Petals falling, a sacred dance,
Inviting all to take a chance.

The Language of Botanical Wishes

In whispers of the leaf,
Wishes flutter, soft and brief.
Petals speak in colors bright,
Dreams alight in morning light.

Roots dig deep, secrets kept,
In the soil, visions crept.
Every seed a silent plea,
In nature's heart, we find the key.

Breezes carry fragrant dreams,
Through gardens filled with silver gleams.
Every flower, a story spun,
In this realm, we are all one.

Underneath the moonlit sky,
Wishes dance and softly sigh.
In the hush of midnight's grace,
We find hope in nature's embrace.

With every bud that dares to grow,
Lives a tale we yearn to know.
In each bloom's gentle sway,
Botanical wishes find their way.

Garden of Ethereal Visions

Amongst the shadows cool and deep,
Ethereal visions softly creep.
A garden built on dreams yet born,
Where stars repose, and wishes mourn.

Suspended in a silken breeze,
Thoughts commune beneath the trees.
Fleeting moments whisper here,
In the stillness, all is clear.

Colors blend like sunset hues,
Guiding hearts to gentle views.
Petals fold like hands in prayer,
Beckoning a world more fair.

In every corner, silence dwells,
Among fragrant blooms, time swells.
Each sigh of wind a promise kept,
Where sleep and dreams in stillness slept.

Footsteps echo in the night,
Unveiling paths of pure delight.
In this garden, visions share,
A tapestry of hope laid bare.

When Thoughts Take Root

In fertile lands where silence reigns,
Thoughts take root, break unseen chains.
Teeming dreams beneath the ground,
Awakening, rich earth's profound.

Each idea, a slender shoot,
Stretching high, seeking fruit.
In the warmth of sun's embrace,
Every whisper finds its place.

Watering with a gentle hand,
Nurturing dreams, like grains of sand.
In the stillness, seeds commune,
Finding light from sun and moon.

Beneath the surface, stories grow,
Roots intertwine, and feelings flow.
A tapestry of echoing hopes,
In this realm, ambition copes.

As seasons shift and time unfolds,
Nature breathes, its wisdom holds.
When thoughts take root in earth's embrace,
They blossom forth, a sacred space.

The Scent of Infinite Horizons

In valleys lush where spirits soar,
The scent of horizons calls to explore.
Every breeze a tale unfolds,
Of journeys vast, of dreams retold.

Morning dew on petals bright,
Whispers of paths bathed in light.
Across the fields, a fragrant promise,
Eternity held within its solemnness.

The air alive with fragrant lore,
Encouraging hearts to seek for more.
Every step unveils a treasure,
In scents of life, we find our measure.

Beyond the hills, where sunlight streams,
Exist endless possibilities, endless dreams.
In the caress of nature's breath,
We find the essence that conquers death.

With every bloom that graces time,
The scent of horizons becomes our rhyme.
In nature's arms, we find a way,
To chase the dawn of a new day.

Raindrops of Enchanted Flora

Raindrops dance on leaves so green,
Nature's jewels in sunlight's sheen.
Each droplet sings a quiet song,
Of growth and beauty, ever strong.

Whispers breathe through gentle breeze,
Caressing blooms with sweet release.
Colors awaken, hearts aligned,
In this world where dreams unwind.

Petals shimmer with playful grace,
Reflecting joy in every space.
With every drop, life starts anew,
A canvas painted in vibrant hue.

Among the roots, the earth will sigh,
As rain urges the blooms to rise high.
In this garden of soft delight,
Magic blooms in morning light.

Echoing through the tranquil vale,
Each raindrop weaves a tender tale.
Of enchanted flora, bold and bright,
Their essence caught in nature's light.

Bursting with Vibrant Potential

In the dawn, the colors explode,
Each hue a story yet untold.
Dreams awaken from slumber deep,
In the promise that they keep.

With every petal that unfolds,
A world of wonder more than gold.
Leaves whisper secrets of the day,
In vibrant strokes of nature's play.

Roots grasp tight the earth below,
While branches stretch to skies aglow.
Potential blooms in every heart,
Waiting patiently to take part.

Life is painted in strokes so bold,
With fervent tales of hopes retold.
Bursting forth like spring's bright sun,
In every moment, we are one.

Beneath the surface, currents flow,
A tapestry of dreams to sow.
Together, we rise, strong and free,
In a vibrant dance of destiny.

The Colorful Whirl of Possibilities

In a swirl of colors bright,
Possibilities take their flight.
Each shade a pathway yet to roam,
Inviting dreams to find their home.

The canvas spins, a joyful race,
With every twist, we find our place.
Each turn ignites the spark within,
In this kaleidoscope we spin.

Blooming thoughts like flowers burst,
The rich expanse of creative thirst.
In every hue, a story waits,
To be untangled by our fates.

Whirling freely through the air,
With laughter echoing everywhere.
Life unfolds in vibrant schemes,
A colorful dance of our dreams.

Each breath we take is laced with hope,
As we embrace the way to cope.
In this colorful whirl, we belong,
Together, we weave a wondrous song.

Secrets Written in Petal Scripts

Beneath the blooms, a tale is spun,
In every petal, secrets run.
Whispers of love and dreams untold,
In fragile forms, their truths unfold.

The language of the flowers speaks,
In written scripts, it softly creeks.
Each color carries hidden lore,
In nature's heart, we long for more.

Delicate scents and patterns fine,
Entwined in stories, yours and mine.
Fragrance of memory, faint yet clear,
In every bloom, a wish held dear.

Rustling leaves in quiet grace,
Paint vivid stories, time can't erase.
Possibilities in every line,
A canvas waiting, so divine.

With gentle hands, we trace the scripts,
Each petal witnesses our trips.
In nature's book, we find our role,
Secrets stitched in petals' soul.

Radiance Beneath the Moonlit Canopy

Underneath the silver glow,
Whispers dance in night's soft breeze,
Leaves shiver with secrets low,
As shadows weave through ancient trees.

Stars twinkle like distant dreams,
Guiding hearts through the quiet night,
Moonlight paints the world in gleams,
As nature sings in pure delight.

Softly glows the forest floor,
With magic wrapped in twilight's cloak,
Every rustle, every roar,
A symphony where silence spoke.

Paths of light lead us on,
In this realm where spirits play,
Where the night will soon be gone,
And dawn breaks the spell to day.

Beneath the heavens, shadows blend,
A place where dreams forever twine,
In the moon's embrace, we transcend,
Finding solace, hearts align.

Voyage Through the Colorful Veil

Colors swirl in swirling sheets,
A canvas bright with life and cheer,
Through the sky, the day retreats,
As hues of sunset soften near.

Waves of amber, crimson dream,
Flow across the endless sea,
Each stroke recalls a hidden gleam,
In this voyage, we roam free.

Tales of journeys, skies so vast,
In the petals of the dawn,
Every moment, memories cast,
While the vibrant day is drawn.

Clouds brush the heavens with their grace,
Mirroring the heart's own glow,
In this dance, find sacred space,
Where time fades to ebb and flow.

Through the colors, dreams unfurl,
Every shadow bright and bold,
In this tapestry, we twirl,
Finding magic in colors told.

When Blossoms Call the Stars

Petals fall like gentle snow,
In gardens where the night unfolds,
Whispers linger, sweet and slow,
As each flower's story told.

Underneath a velvet sky,
Blossoms reach for heavenly light,
Swaying softly as they sigh,
In the tender arms of night.

Stars awaken, twinkle bright,
Drawing dreams upon the earth,
In their glow, all feels so right,
For every blossom holds rebirth.

Echoes of a springtime dance,
Where petals kiss the midnight air,
In this realm, all hearts find chance,
To whisper wishes deep in prayer.

As dawn approaches, shadows flee,
Yet blossoms sing a sweet refrain,
When night returns, once more we see,
Stars call softly, endless gain.

The Enchanted Orchard of Wishes

In the orchard, secrets bloom,
Fruits aglow in softest light,
Wishes whispered, dispel gloom,
As dreams take root in tranquil night.

Branches stretch like open hands,
Cradling hopes on every bough,
In this place where magic stands,
Underneath the moon's soft vow.

Nighttime breezes gently sway,
Carrying the scent of dreams,
Each petal dreams of brighter days,
While starlight dances, winks, and beams.

A pathway leads to secret springs,
Where laughter mingles with delight,
Among the trees, the heart still sings,
In the glow of magic night.

Embrace the wonder, hold it tight,
Within this orchard's warm embrace,
Let every wish take flight tonight,
In enchanted joy, find your place.

Reveries Painted in Color

Brush strokes of dreams in the air,
Whispers of hues that dance without care.
Canvas of thoughts, vivid and bright,
Imagined worlds bathed in pure light.

Brushes dipped deep in the soul,
Filling the void to make us whole.
Every shade tells a story untold,
In the gallery of memories bold.

Palettes of passion spilling wide,
Flooded with joy, nowhere to hide.
Each color a heartbeat, a sigh,
In a tapestry where dreams can fly.

Swirls of laughter, splashes of grace,
Filling each corner of time and space.
Reveries painted in endless hue,
A world reborn, vibrant and true.

Beneath the Silvered Dew

Morning's first kiss through leaves so green,
Awakening life, a soft sheen.
Silvered droplets on petals gleam,
A whispering song, nature's own dream.

Tranquil moments wrapped in still air,
Each breath a treasure, beyond compare.
Nature's embrace in gentle sway,
Guiding the heart to greet the day.

Through whispered winds and rustling trees,
We find our peace, our worries cease.
Beneath the silver, life takes its flight,
In a world woven with pure delight.

Sunrise unfolding, painting the sky,
Colors emerge as shadows say goodbye.
Beneath the silvered dew we stand,
In the quiet moments, hand in hand.

Garden of the Mind's Delights

In a garden lush where thoughts grow wild,
Imagination blooms, free and unstyled.
Petals of wisdom, fragrant and bright,
Whispering secrets in soft moonlight.

Paths intertwine like dreams in a haze,
Guiding the wanderer through life's maze.
Each flower tells tales of joy and strife,
In the quiet corners, memories rife.

Butterflies flutter, yearning to soar,
Echoing laughter from days of yore.
Each rustling leaf shares a sacred prayer,
In this garden of thoughts, love fills the air.

Sunlight spills warmth on a canvas wide,
Creating a haven where hopes abide.
In the garden, the mind takes flight,
Where vision blossoms, forever bright.

Echoes of Serenity in Bloom

In tranquil gardens, peace unfolds,
Echoes of silence, a story told.
Petals unfurl in soft embrace,
Whispers of nature fill the space.

Gentle breezes, a lullaby's song,
Guiding lost souls where they belong.
Each heartbeat resonant, deep and true,
In the stillness, a world anew.

Ripples of calm in the evening light,
Filling the heart, bringing delight.
Every moment a shimmering pearl,
In the tapestry of this wondrous swirl.

As twilight descends, colors ignite,
Painting the skies in soft twilight.
Echoes of serenity, life's sweet tune,
In harmony's arms, we eternally swoon.

Whispers of Petal Skies

In the calm of twilight's sweep,
Petals dance with secrets deep,
Beneath a sky soft and wide,
Whispers weave where dreams abide.

Gentle breezes carry sound,
Of echoes lost, yet softly found,
Each bloom sings in hues of grace,
Painting love in a warm embrace.

The twilight hush, a tender hush,
Brings forth colors, the heart's soft blush,
As twilight melts to night's embrace,
Petal whispers find their place.

Stars blink softly, skies will share,
Dreamy tales in fragrant air,
While moonlight drapes in silver threads,
On gardens where our love treads.

Each petal holds a timeless truth,
Of tender hearts and blooming youth,
In the whispers of the skies,
Love in nature never dies.

Awakening in Color

Morning light breaks through the haze,
Colors dance in perfect praise,
Awakening the world anew,
With brushstrokes bold in every hue.

Leaves unfurl in glistening gold,
Stories of the sun retold,
Each petal glows, a vibrant sight,
As nature wakes to the warm light.

Birds sing sweet in morning's arms,
Nature's symphony, a million charms,
Life bursts forth in vivid spree,
Awakening calls from land to sea.

Colors merge in the dawning glow,
A canvas bright with beauty's flow,
Each heartbeat synchronized with bliss,
Love is found in every kiss.

Awakening holds a timeless grace,
In every blossom's warm embrace,
As hues collide, our spirits blend,
In colors bright, our dreams ascend.

The Garden of Reverie

In the garden where dreams unfold,
Beneath skies painted with gold,
Whispers linger, soft and light,
In a world where hearts take flight.

Petals curl like lovers' sighs,
In this space where time flies,
Each blossom holds a memory dear,
Echoing laughter, sweet and clear.

Among the greens, the blues entwine,
In every shade, a hint divine,
The fragrance wraps like softest threads,
In the garden where our hope spreads.

Through winding paths and hidden nooks,
A tapestry in nature's books,
Each moment, a treasure to keep,
In the garden where we dream deep.

With hands intertwined, we roam,
In this sacred space, we find home,
In every bloom, in every sigh,
The garden whispers sweet goodbye.

Echoes of Blossoming Thoughts

In the silence of the dawn,
Thoughts arise, like blooms drawn,
Each whisper gentle, soft, and clear,
Echoes found in nature's sphere.

Moments linger, soft and sweet,
With every breath, our hearts repeat,
The song of life, a rhythmic flow,
In thoughts that bloom, like flowers grow.

Underneath a sky of dreams,
Hope glimmers in sunlit beams,
A tapestry of woven grace,
In blooming thoughts, our souls embrace.

Each petal holds a tale untold,
Of whispered fears and courage bold,
In every echo, a vision clear,
A garden where our dreams appear.

Echoes fade, but truths remain,
In the unfolding of joy and pain,
Thoughts will blossom, hearts will find,
In nature's arms, we're intertwined.

A Tapestry of Fantasies

In the weave of dreams, we find our way,
Colorful threads in bright display.
Whispers of hope in every hue,
A dance of wonders, old and new.

Stars stitched softly on the night,
Guiding hearts with gentle light.
Every stitch a story told,
In this fabric, brave and bold.

A loom of wishes, spun with care,
Through tiny gaps, our secrets share.
Each pattern holds a wish unfurled,
A magic tapestry of our world.

Where fantasies meet, realities part,
Boundless visions that touch the heart.
In every fold, a dream takes flight,
A journey crafted from pure delight.

Together we weave, in joy and strife,
A tapestry bright, depicting life.
Stitch by stitch, side by side,
In this fantasy, we forever reside.

Fragrant Wishes Unleashed

In a garden lush with scents divine,
Petals open to the sun's warm shine.
Each bloom whispers secrets sweet,
In fragrant wishes, hearts do meet.

Tendrils of hope in the gentle breeze,
Carried softly through swaying trees.
With every sigh, a new dream starts,
Fragrant wishes fill our hearts.

Lavender hues and rose's blush,
They beckon softly, hush and hush.
In the air, a promise made,
A symphony of lives displayed.

Breezes swirl in a playful dance,
Inviting us to take a chance.
With every scent that wraps around,
Fragrant wishes are found and bound.

In twilight's glow, they stir and rise,
Dancing lightly beneath the skies.
Each longing lifted, each hope released,
In this garden, our souls are eased.

Garden of Serendipity

Beneath the arch of blooming trees,
A garden hums with secret pleas.
In every leaf, a chance to find,
The beauty born from hearts entwined.

Where laughter floats on sunlit air,
And winding paths lead anywhere.
The petals beckon us to stay,
In this serendipitous display.

A tapestry of life unfolds,
In gentle whispers, stories told.
With every step, new dreams arise,
Serendipity inspires the skies.

Butterflies dance from flower to flower,
As time weaves on, hour by hour.
In this enchanted place we roam,
A garden blooms, our hearts find home.

In unexpected turns, we find delight,
In shadows cast by soft twilight.
A sanctuary for souls in flight,
In this garden, all feels right.

Where Shadows Embrace the Light

In twilight's glow, the shadows play,
They gather close, then drift away.
A gentle dance of dark and bright,
Where shadows embrace the light.

Among the trees, the silence speaks,
In hushed tones where the spirit seeks.
Every flicker, a story spins,
In the quiet where hope begins.

Moonlit whispers grace the night,
As stars peek out, a wondrous sight.
In this moment, fear takes flight,
Where shadows embrace the light.

Every heartbeat, a sacred claim,
A spark ignited, a flickering flame.
In the interplay between day and night,
We dance in shadows, holding tight.

With each dawn, the shadows fade,
Yet in their depth, our dreams are laid.
In the dance where love ignites,
Our spirits soar, embracing light.

Starlit Garden of the Heart

In shadows cast by silver light,
Whispers dance through the night,
Petals gleam with dewy grace,
In love's embrace, we find our place.

Beneath the stars, dreams take flight,
A symphony of pure delight,
Fleeting moments, soft and sweet,
In this garden, our hearts meet.

With every bloom, a secret shared,
In fragrant air, we're unprepared,
Time stands still as we explore,
Each heartbeat opens a new door.

Laughter floats on the evening breeze,
As nature cracks its melodies,
Hand in hand, we roam the ways,
In starlit whispers, our love plays.

So let us wander, heart to heart,
In this garden, we'll never part,
For in the night, we both shall see,
The starlit love that sets us free.

Fragrant Fantasies Unfurled

In the morning's gentle light,
Blossoms wake from the night,
Each petal holds a whispered dream,
Life unfolds like a tender beam.

Fragrant herbs and blooms awake,
While butterflies dance and partake,
In gardens where hopes intertwine,
Moments crafted, pure, divine.

The sun smiles down, a golden hue,
As colors burst in vibrant view,
Every scent a tale retold,
Of beauty cherished, never old.

With every step, the soul ignites,
In fragrant realms, our hearts take flights,
Connecting threads of joy and pain,
In fragrant fantasies, we remain.

So let the blossoms freely sway,
In dreams of love, we find our way,
Through fragrant paths, we twirl and dance,
In nature's spell, we're lost in chance.

Petals Beneath the Twilight

As twilight drapes the earth in gold,
Petals whisper tales of old,
Secrets wrapped in twilight's hue,
Beneath the sky, we craft anew.

In quiet corners, shadows play,
While stars begin their nightly sway,
Each breath becomes a timeless song,
In gentle twilight, where we belong.

Softly now, the night unfolds,
As silver dreams begin to hold,
A tapestry of lush repose,
In twilight's arms, our passion grows.

Here, under skies that softly gleam,
We lose ourselves in tender dreams,
With every petal, hopes take flight,
In this embrace, all feels so right.

So let the dusk paint our delight,
With whispers shared in fading light,
Petals rest beneath the vine,
In twilight's breath, our souls entwine.

Rise of the Midnight Flora

When darkness wraps the world so tight,
A hidden bloom ignites the night,
In shadows deep, a secret dance,
Of midnight flowers, lost in trance.

Silhouettes in a moonlit haze,
Emerging soft from twilight's glaze,
Each blossom glows, a silent wish,
In the heart of night, they find their bliss.

The air fills with an ancient song,
As whispers beckon the lost along,
To where the midnight secrets lie,
In every petal, dreams comply.

Here we wander, hand in hand,
In this enchanted, darkened land,
Where flowers thrive in silken night,
Their colors bold, their spirits bright.

So let us greet this sacred hour,
Together, bloom like midnight flower,
In every heartbeat, we'll arise,
Bound by love 'neath endless skies.

The Influence of Flourishing Thoughts

In the garden of the mind, ideas grow,
Bright like petals, swaying to and fro.
Nurtured by sunlight, watered with care,
Each thought a flower, blooming everywhere.

Whispers of wisdom drift on the breeze,
Painting visions in the rustling leaves.
With roots entwined, our dreams take flight,
In a world where hope glows ever bright.

Morning dew kisses the vibrant hues,
Each drop a promise, in shades of blues.
Pollinators dance, spread the news wide,
Of flourishing thoughts that cannot hide.

Through storms and shadows, they learn to thrive,
In the depths of darkness, they jive and strive.
With every season, they find new ways,
Transforming the nights into dazzling days.

So tend to your garden, let passion sway,
Harvest the dreams that blossom each day.
For in the influence of thoughts that bloom,
A radiant future dispels all gloom.

The Stargazer's Botanical Escape

Under a veil of stars, I roam free,
Lost in the cosmos, just my soul and me.
A dance of lights paint the evening sky,
Whispers of nature, a gentle sigh.

Among the moonlit petals that softly gleam,
I find a solace that feels like a dream.
Each flower's whisper, a tale of old,
In the night's embrace, their secrets unfold.

Constellations twinkle above my head,
Guiding my footsteps where shadows tread.
With every bloom, a story arrayed,
In the starlit garden where peace is laid.

The fragrance of jasmine lifts me high,
As I chase the echoes of stars in the sky.
With the world below, so vast and deep,
In this floral haven, my heart leaps.

So, let me wander through this celestial space,
The stargazer's heart finds a soft embrace.
In nature's arms, my spirit awakes,
In the botanical realms that the nighttime makes.

Chasing the Blooms of Imagination

In a field of dreams, I wander and run,
Chasing the blooms, kissed by the sun.
Vibrant colors burst, each petal a spark,
A tapestry woven in the light and dark.

Whispers of fantasy float on the air,
Tales of wonder, beyond compare.
A quicksilver moment, the heart ignites,
As blooms of imagination take flight.

Fragrant aspirations line the bright path,
Each step revealing joy's bubbled laugh.
With every twist, a new dream appears,
Unfurling stories across the years.

From morning glories to daffodils bold,
Each natural wonder, a tale to be told.
In the garden of thought, I plant and sow,
Chasing the blooms that help me to grow.

So let the colors paint my sky wide,
With petals of vision, and dreams as my guide.
In this boundless space where imagination thrives,
Life's sweetest moments are where love survives.

Petals of Memory Floating

In the quiet moments, memories drift,
Like petals scattered, a tender gift.
Each one a story, a glimpse of the past,
In the heart's repository, forever cast.

Whispers of laughter float on the breeze,
Echoing softly through the ancient trees.
Every petal dances, a silent refrain,
Reminding me gently of joy and of pain.

Colors of yesteryear paint my mind,
In the garden of now, the past intertwined.
Fragrant reminders of love once known,
Like autumn leaves, no longer alone.

As I gather the petals, I make a bouquet,
Of cherished moments that never decay.
In the layers of time, I find my place,
In shadows and light, memory's embrace.

So let the rain fall, let the winds blow,
For in every petal, my heart tends to grow.
In this floral memory floating in space,
I find timeless beauty, an eternal grace.

The Mysterious Dance of Colors

In shadows deep, the colors blend,
Whispers of hues that never end.
Each stroke a pulse, a silent call,
In every corner, magic enthralls.

The twilight sings, a vibrant tune,
As the stars embrace the whispering moon.
Shades of crimson and hints of blue,
Converging dreams in a wondrous view.

Twisting spectrums in gentle sway,
A canvas alive, come dance and play.
The brush in hand, a heart set free,
In this ballet of mystery.

Glimmers spark in the fading light,
Echoes of shadows take flight in the night.
A secret path through each painted lane,
Where colors and silence weave joy and pain.

A world unfolds, vibrant and bright,
In the embrace of magical night.
Together we soar on this vivid line,
In the dance of colors, forever entwined.

Blossoms of the Hidden Heart

In the garden where secrets bloom,
Whispers linger, dispelling gloom.
Petals soft, in shades of grace,
Awakening love in a sacred space.

Beneath the leaves, a heartbeat stirs,
Each flower sings of untold furors.
A fragrance sweet, a tale to tell,
Of dreams encased in a floral shell.

In morning dew, the truth appears,
A gentle touch to calm our fears.
The blossoms sway in tender light,
A dance of shadows in flight.

Crimson and gold in harmony,
Reflecting hope, a symphony.
The hidden heart, unbound and free,
In every bloom, find our decree.

In every petal, wisdom lies,
Under the vast and boundless skies.
Together we cherish this fleeting art,
The blossoms sing of the hidden heart.

Embracing the Floral Whisper

In twilight's hush, the flowers speak,
Each gentle breeze, a secret peak.
Softly blooming, their stories unfold,
In the rustling green, their tales told.

A garden's sigh, a fragrant breeze,
Where silence dances among the trees.
Petals drift like whispered dreams,
Flowing lightly on sunlit streams.

In shades of lavender and bright yellow,
The harmony found in nature's hello.
Embracing each color, a delicate grace,
In every flower, a warm embrace.

The whispers linger as night descends,
In the moonlight's glow, the spirit mends.
A tapestry woven of scent and glow,
In floral embrace, let the heart grow.

So join the dance, let your soul unfurl,
In the gentle sway of the floral whirl.
For in each whisper, a truth so clear,
We find our peace, our home, our sphere.

A Bouquet of Unraveled Thoughts

In tangled threads, ideas collide,
A bouquet of thoughts where dreams reside.
Colors entwined in harmony's grace,
Each blossom holds a unique place.

Petals of laughter, stems of desire,
Thoughts blooming high, like a blazing fire.
Nurtured by hopes in morning light,
A tapestry woven, pure and bright.

In fragrant whispers, the mind takes flight,
Exploring the depths of day and night.
Each bloom a story, vivid and bold,
Unraveling truths the heart longs to hold.

As seasons change, ideas will morph,
The bouquet grows, seeking new north.
Embrace the chaos, the beauty unfurls,
A dance of thoughts in a vibrant swirl.

So gather your dreams, let them take root,
In a garden of thoughts, let life shoot.
For in each bloom lies a treasure sought,
A bouquet of unspoken thoughts.

Kaleidoscope of Enchanted Landscapes

In valleys lush where shadows play,
The colors dance, bright as the day.
Mountains rise with dreams in sight,
A canvas painted with pure delight.

Rivers weave through emerald fields,
Nature's bounty gently yields.
Whispers of winds in the trees,
A symphony of rustling leaves.

Sunsets spill in hues divine,
Gold and crimson intertwine.
Stars awaken in twilight's sigh,
Their twinkle hints of thoughts that fly.

Paths of wonder twist and turn,
With every bend, new lessons learned.
Magic lingers in the air,
Inviting souls to wander, dare.

In every corner, beauty found,
In silence deep, and lively sound.
A kaleidoscope, forever bright,
Enchanted landscapes, pure delight.

Echoes in the Blooming Wilderness

The meadow breathes in fragrant hues,
With wildflowers that chase the blues.
Honeybees in joyful flight,
Whisper secrets, day and night.

Mountains echo distant calls,
As ancient history gently falls.
Footsteps follow nature's beat,
In harmony, where spirits meet.

Tales of old in rustling grass,
Time stood still, yet moments pass.
Beneath the trees, a story's spun,
In blooming wilderness, all is one.

With every petal, shadows blend,
In this place where dreams ascend.
Whispers linger, softly stirred,
Echoes of a sacred word.

Through the wild, our hearts take flight,
In the warmth of the fading light.
Nature holds us, wild and free,
In echoes that call to you and me.

The Symphony of Floral Whispers

In gardens where the blossoms sigh,
Petals fall like whispers nigh.
A symphony on nature's stage,
With fragrant notes that never age.

Lilies swaying, soft and fair,
Compose a melody in the air.
Sunflowers turn to follow light,
A dance of joy, pure and bright.

Roses bloom with tales untold,
Each bloom a secret, pure and bold.
Violets twinkle, shy and small,
In nature's song, we hear them all.

Lavender drifts on breezes sweet,
In every note, our hearts compete.
Daisies nod in gentle sway,
Creating harmonies each day.

With every breath, a flower speaks,
An orchestra in soft mystique.
In the garden's endless dance,
Floral whispers weave romance.

Embrace of the Night's Garden

As twilight falls, the garden glows,
In shadows deep where stillness flows.
Moonlight spills on petals bright,
Embracing dreams within the night.

Night-blooming jasmine, sweet and rare,
Shares secrets with the midnight air.
Crickets chant a soothing tune,
Underneath the watchful moon.

Stars twinkle in a velvet sky,
Guiding hearts that wander by.
In the hush, the world retreats,
While every pulse of magic beats.

With fireflies dancing, shadows play,
The night reveals its hidden way.
A symphony of light and dark,
In every corner, a timeless spark.

Through rose and thorn, in soft embrace,
We find our place in nature's grace.
A garden whispers, pure and true,
In night's embrace, it waits for you.

Whispers of the Midnight Garden

In shadows deep, the secrets play,
Beneath the moon's soft silver ray.
A breeze that stirs the fragrant night,
Whispers of dreams take gentle flight.

The flowers bloom, their colors rare,
Clad in the dew, a fragrant air.
With every sigh, the night unfolds,
Stories of love the garden holds.

Stars twinkle high with a watchful gaze,
As twilight deepens, the magic stays.
Each petal's touch, a tender grace,
In this enchanted, sacred space.

A rustle here, a laughter there,
Nature hums a tune so fair.
The nightingale sings soft and low,
In whispers that the heart will know.

As dawn approaches, dreams take flight,
The garden fades in morning light.
Yet in our hearts, the whispers gleam,
A lasting echo of the dream.

Petals of Hope Unfurled

From tiny seeds, great gardens grow,
With every raindrop, life will flow.
Beneath the sun, the flowers rise,
Petals of hope reach for the skies.

In colors bright, they dance with glee,
A vibrant sight, a melody.
Each gentle breeze shares tales anew,
Of dreams once lost and hopes pursued.

The earth awakens from its sleep,
Through cracks in stone, the roots will creep.
A tender bud, a story starts,
With every bloom, it warms the hearts.

In the quiet dusk, shadows fall,
Soft fragrance lingers, nature's call.
The nightingale sings of dreams unfurled,
In petals bright, a hopeful world.

When winter comes, and frost holds tight,
The seeds remember, beneath the night.
In spring's embrace, they will return,
To weave their magic, hearts will yearn.

The Awakening Blossom

A single bud in morning light,
Stirs from slumber, a lovely sight.
With petals closed, it holds its breath,
Awaits the sun, defying death.

As warmth caresses, colors bloom,
In gentle arcs, dispelling gloom.
The world around begins to wake,
In softest hues, the hearts will ache.

Each passing hour, the dance unfolds,
With whispers sweet, the tale is told.
A tapestry of life's embrace,
In fragrant air, there's peace and grace.

In evening's hush, the day retreats,
The blossom glows, the fragrance sweet.
It whispers tales of paths once crossed,
Of love found, and dreams not lost.

As day gives way to velvet night,
The flower closes, holding tight.
In every cycle, life goes on,
In waking dreams, we all belong.

Laughter Beneath the Starlit Canopy

Under the stars, we gather near,
With laughter bright, and hearts sincere.
Each twinkling light, a story told,
Of friendships forged, and secrets bold.

The moonlight dances on our faces,
In this enchanted, sacred place.
With every giggle, warmth does grow,
As dreams take flight on night's soft glow.

A whispered joke, a playful tease,
Within the night, our spirits ease.
In this embrace, we find our peace,
Under the stars, our joy won't cease.

The night unfolds, a magic tune,
As fireflies twirl beneath the moon.
With hands entwined, we share the gaze,
Lost in the glow of twilight haze.

In laughter's echo, bonds will form,
A tapestry of love, so warm.
Beneath the stars, we pledge to be,
Together always, wild and free.

Secrets of the Flowering Mind

In whispers soft, the petals sway,
A tale of thoughts in bloom today.
Where dreams unfurl in colors bright,
The heart reveals its inner light.

Each secret stirs, like morning dew,
Awakening the world anew.
With every breath, a dance, a chance,
In nature's trance, the mind does prance.

A garden wild, a maze of care,
Where joy and sorrow blend the air.
In hidden depths, the wisdom lies,
A universe within each sigh.

The blooming thoughts, like stars at night,
Illuminate the dark with light.
In silence deep, the answers flow,
A river vast where feelings grow.

With every glance, the soul takes flight,
In harmony, the day and night.
Secrets shared with every breeze,
The flowering mind feels at ease.

The Horizon's Soft Embrace

Beyond the waves, where sky meets sea,
In twilight's glow, I long to be.
Where shadows dance on golden sand,
A gentle touch from nature's hand.

Each sunset paints the world apart,
With hues that soothe the restless heart.
The horizon whispers soft and low,
In every tale the breezes blow.

The clouds they wander, free and vast,
They carry dreams from future past.
In fading light, the stars appear,
A promise made, forever near.

In twilight's arms, I find my peace,
As day gives way, my worries cease.
The sky a canvas, love's embrace,
In every shade, I find my place.

With every breath, the twilight sings,
Of all the hope a new day brings.
The horizon calls, my spirit soars,
In soft embrace, my heart explores.

Celestial Seeds of Longing

In starlit dreams, the seeds are sown,
A yearning deep, but never known.
Each twinkling light, a wish in flight,
Guides the heart through the endless night.

With every pulse, each beat, each breath,
The cosmos dances with life and death.
The longing grows, like vines entwined,
In the garden of the seeking mind.

The nightingale sings a sorrowed song,
Of lost connections that feel so wrong.
In every note, a whisper fades,
Of love once known in twilight glades.

Celestial seeds in silence wait,
For whispers soft to navigate.
In dreams they sprout, beneath the stars,
A tapestry of hidden scars.

So let them bloom in gentle grace,
As time reveals each sacred place.
With every wish, the light will grow,
In the heart's embrace, the true seeds flow.

Vivid Horizons

In shades of blue, the day begins,
Infinity where dreaming spins.
The horizon beckons with a smile,
Inviting all to stay awhile.

With every step on golden ground,
The magic rises all around.
In vibrant hues, the spirit flies,
Awakening the sunlit skies.

Beneath the trees, where whispers play,
The world transforms in bright array.
Each path I choose, each turn I take,
A vivid dance, no fear to break.

With eyes that see the beauty near,
The joy of life is ever clear.
In every moment, every glance,
The vivid dreams ignite the chance.

Horizons stretch, both near and far,
A universe, where wonders are.
Embrace the light that brightly shows,
In vivid heart, the journey grows.

Endless Possibilities

A canvas wide, a world unchained,
Each thought a brush, unrestrained.
In colors bright, our stories start,
Endless dreams from the beating heart.

The paths we walk, the roads unknown,
With every choice, the seeds are sown.
In every twist, a chance to see,
The endless possibilities.

With open minds, we chase the dawn,
With every ending, a new song drawn.
In laughter shared, or sorrow's plight,
Every moment spins its light.

From shadows cast, new futures rise,
In every dawn, the spark ignites.
A symphony of hope unfolds,
In stories new, our fate extols.

So take my hand, let's journey far,
Through uncharted lands, beneath the stars.
For in our hearts, the truth we seek,
Endless possibilities, a world unique.

Wonders of the Botanical Imagination

In the garden where colors blend,
Petals whisper tales that transcend.
Each leaf tells stories soft and bright,
In the depths of the day and the hush of night.

Roots entwined in silent dreams,
Nature's canvas bursting at the seams.
Underneath the sky, wonders awaken,
Imagination blooms, never forsaken.

The fragrance of hope fills the air,
Every bud a promise, vibrant and rare.
In this realm of rich delight,
Beauty sways, a pure insight.

Among the ferns, secrets lie,
Whispers of the earth and sky.
With every sigh, a new world grows,
Through the thickets, a river flows.

In the twilight, shadows gleam,
Nature's wonder is but a dream.
With every bloom, a heart can mend,
In this garden, life transcends.

The Sleep of Enchanted Meadows

Among the daisies, softly curled,
Gentle dreams of nature swirled.
The sun dips low, the sky a blaze,
As twilight sighs in golden haze.

Silence blankets the evening dew,
With whispers of night, calm and true.
In hidden corners, shadows play,
As the meadow bids farewell to day.

Crickets serenade from afar,
Under the watch of a silver star.
The flowers bask in moonlit glow,
Dreams unfold where the breezes blow.

In slumber's embrace, time stands still,
The world asleep, all dreams fulfill.
Enchantments linger, soft and light,
In the meadows, all is right.

With each breath, the earth reveals,
A tapestry of life that heals.
Bathed in peace, a soft refrain,
In enchanted meadows, joy remains.

Flora's Hidden Promises

In the forest where shadows weave,
Life's gentle secrets start to cleave.
Every bloom holds tales untold,
Promises of magic, brave and bold.

Beneath the boughs, wishes lie,
Cradled softly, they grow and sigh.
With each petal, stories comence,
Transformation from silence to immense.

Time weaves a net, subtle and fine,
Connecting hearts through roots entwined.
Amidst the growth, the hopes abide,
In nature's hands, the dreams reside.

With morning light, bright and clear,
Flora whispers what we hold dear.
In the mist, promises dance,
Awakening joy, a sweet romance.

Every garden a sacred tome,
Flora's secrets lead us home.
A promise kept in vibrant hues,
In nature's arms, we can muse.

The Dance of Light Among the Blooms

Sunlight filters through the leaves,
Painting the petals, where beauty breathes.
Golden glimmers on the ground,
In this dance of light, joy is found.

With every step, shadows twirl,
In harmony where colors swirl.
Bees and butterflies join the sight,
In the garden's tender light.

Every flower a radiant beam,
Basking in daylight's gentle dream.
In the breeze, they sway and spin,
Nature's ballet, a joyful din.

The canvas stirs with each soft sigh,
As the sun climbs and the clouds drift by.
Amidst the blooms, life takes its flight,
In the dance of light, pure delight.

With dusk's embrace, the shadows gleam,
As daylight fades, fading the dream.
Yet in each heart, the dance remains,
Light and color, life's sweet gains.